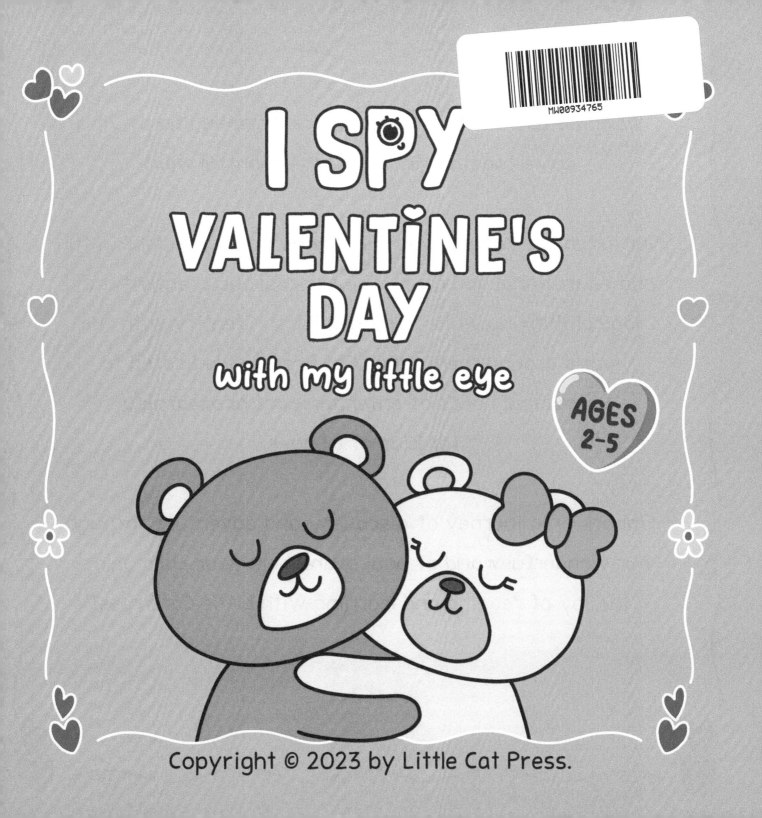

I SPY
VALENTINE'S DAY
with my little eye

AGES 2-5

Welcome to Little Cat Press, where learning and playing come together in the most delightful way!

Our extensive range of books engage young readers in fun and educational activities. They encourage creativity and logical thinking while helping children identify with the world around them. Little Cat Press is dedicated to providing hours of entertainment and learning for kids of all ages.

Embark on a journey of discovery and adventure through our wonderful world of books, and help your child unlock the joy of reading and learning with Little Cat Press!

LITTLE
CAT
PRESS

HOW TO PLAY

- Find an object in the picture that starts with the given letter.

- Flip the page to see if you're a winner with the answer key.

> HAVE A BLAST! <

THIS BOOK BELONGS TO

_____

_____

_____

I spy with my little eye
something starting with the letter

A

I spy with my little eye
something starting with the letter

B

I spied a **Balloon!**

I spy with my little eye
something starting with the letter

C

I spied a **Chocolate** bar!

I spy with my little eye
something starting with the letter

D

I spied a **Diamond!**

I spy with my little eye
something starting with the letter

E

I spied an **Elephant**!

I spy with my little eye
something starting with the letter

F

I spied a **Fireplace!**

I spy with my little eye
something starting with the letter G

I spied a **Gift** box!

I spy with my little eye
something starting with the letter

H

I spied a **Hat!**

I spy with my little eye
something starting with the letter I

I spied an **Ice Cream!**

I spy with my little eye
something starting with the letter

J

I spied a Jar!

I spy with my little eye
something starting with the letter

K

I spied a **Key**!

I spy with my little eye
something starting with the letter

L

I spied a **Lipstick!**

I spy with my little eye
something starting with the letter **M**

I spied a Mug!

I spy with my little eye
something starting with the letter

N

I spied a **Necklace!**

I spy with my little eye
something starting with the letter

O

I spied an **Owl!**

I spy with my little eye
something starting with the letter P

I spied a **Pillow!**

I spy with my little eye
something starting with the letter

Q

I spied a Quiche!

I spy with my little eye
something starting with the letter

R

I spied a **Ring!**

I spy with my little eye
something starting with the letter

S

I spied a pair of **Sunglasses!**

I spy with my little eye
something starting with the letter

T

I spied a **Tulip**!

I spy with my little eye
something starting with the letter

U

I spied a **Ukulele!**

I spy with my little eye
something starting with the letter

V

I spied a **Violin**!

I spy with my little eye
something starting with the letter

W

I spied a **Watch!**

I spy with my little eye
something starting with the letter

I spied a **Xylophone!**

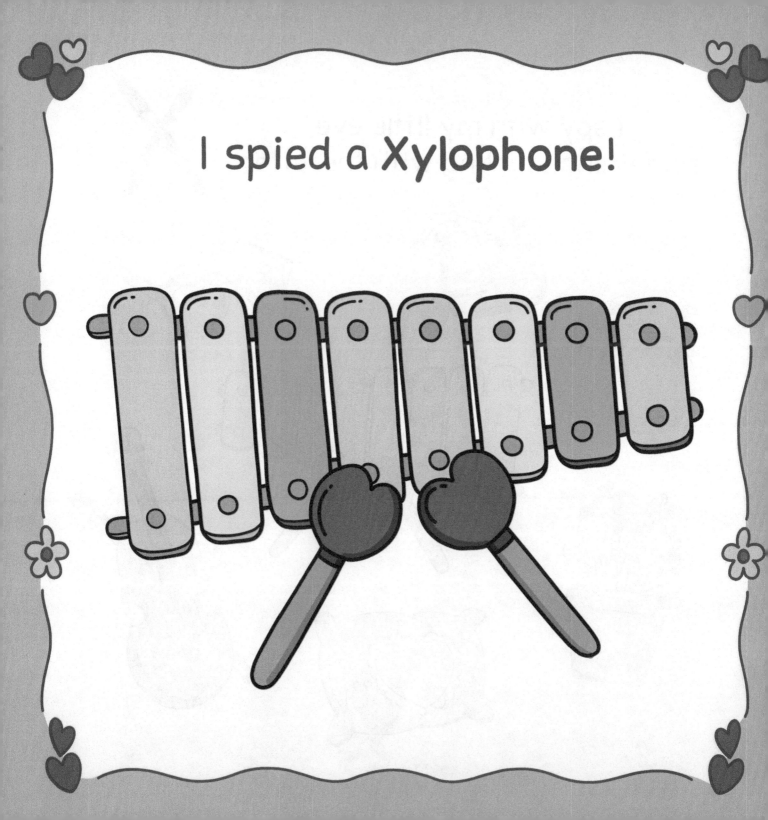

I spy with my little eye
something starting with the letter

Y

I spied a ball of **Yarn!**

Find and count all the cupcakes that look like this one.

There are four cupcakes that look like this one!

Can you find two matching rings?

These two rings look alike!

I spy with my little eye a heart cookie. Can you find it?

Here it is, the heart cookie!

I spy with my little eye a gift box that has a heart shape. Can you find it?

Here it is, the heart-shaped gift box!

Find and count all the ice creams that look like this one.

There are two ice creams that look like this one!

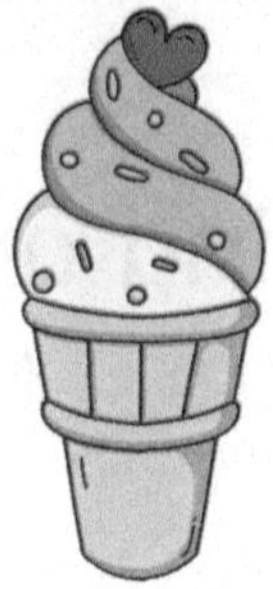

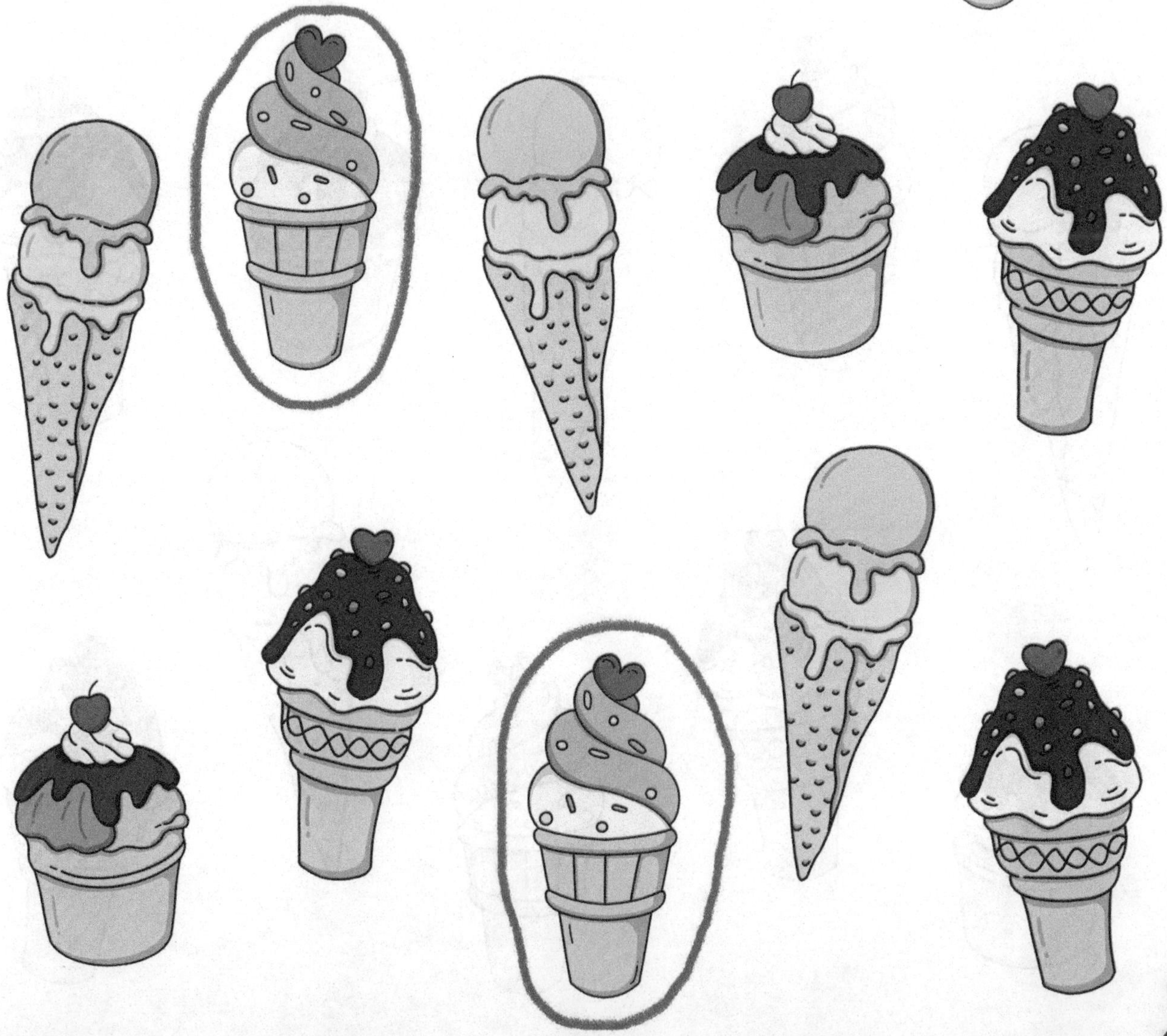

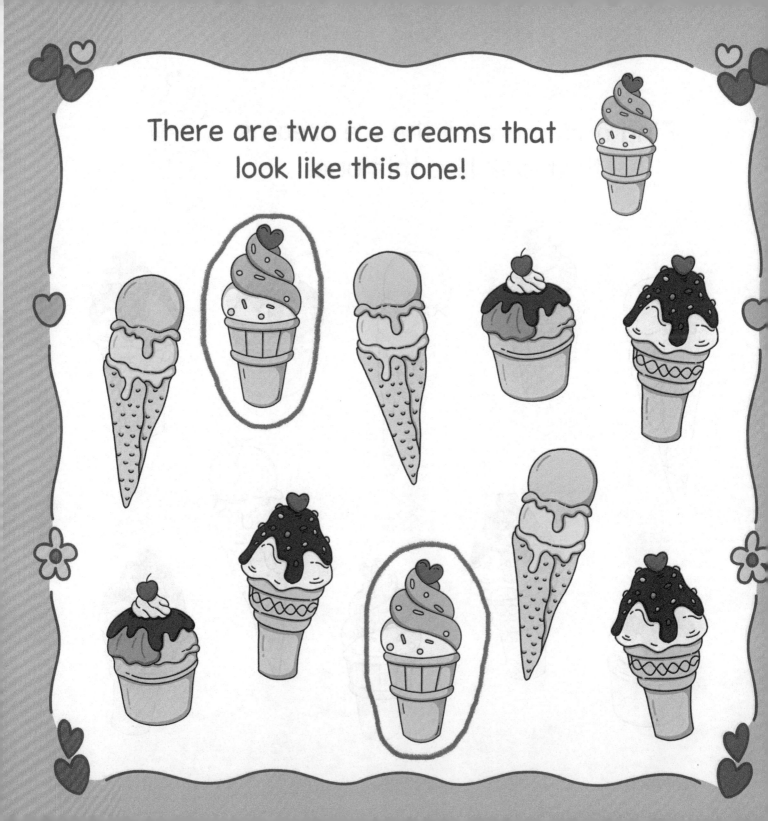

Can you find two jars that look the same?

These two jars look alike!

I spy with my little eye some red tulips.
Can you spot them all?

There are three red tulips in total.

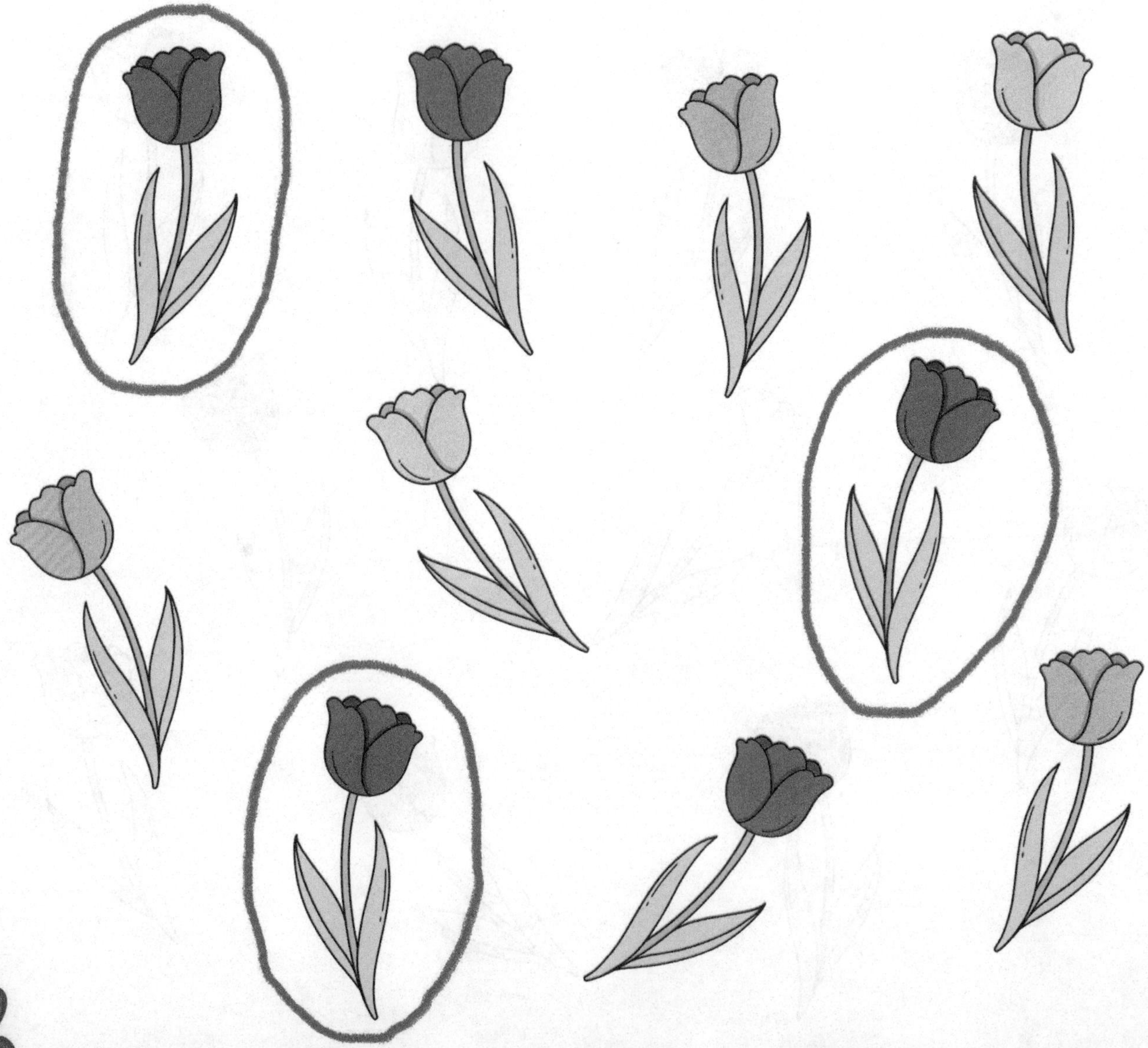

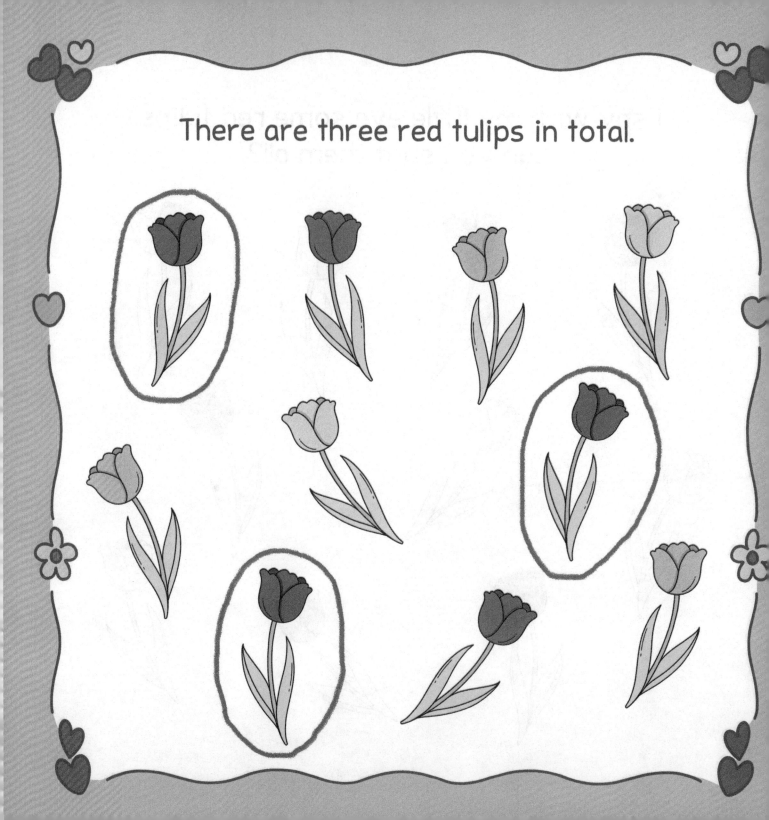

I Spy Valentine's Day

 Angel

 Apron

 Arrow

 Balloon

 Book

 Bouquet

 Cake

 Calendar

 Candle

 Card

 Cheese

 Chocolate

 Cookies

 Cupcake

 Cupid

 Diamond

 Donut

 Dress

 Elephant

 Envelope

 Fireplace

 Gift

 Gnome

 Guitar

 Hat

 Headphones

 Hourglass

 Ice Cream

 Jar

 Key

 Kite

 Lipstick

 Lock

 Love Birds

I Spy Valentine's Day

 Hand Mirror

 Mug

 Necklace

 Octopus

 Owl

 Penguin

 Pillow

 Plant Pot

 Quiche

 Rainbow

 Raspberry

 Ring

 Rose

 Scarf

 Sock

 Sunglasses

 T-shirt

 Teddy Bear

 Tulip

 Ukulele

 Umbrella

 Violin

 Wallet

 Watch

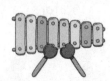 Xylophone

 Yarn

 Yogurt

 Zipper

Made in the USA
Coppell, TX
09 January 2024